Hotel Shadow

Also by Kelvin Corcoran

Robin Hood in the Dark Ages
The Red and Yellow Book
Qiryat Sepher
TCL
The Next Wave
Lyric Lyric
Melanie's Book
When Suzy Was
Your Thinking Tracts or Nations
New and Selected Poems
Roger Hilton's Sugar
Backward Turning Sea

Hotel Shadow

Kelvin Corcoran

Shearsman Books
Exeter

First published in the United Kingdom in 2010 by
Shearsman Books Ltd
58 Velwell Road
Exeter EX4 4LD

www.shearsman.com

ISBN 978-1-84861-142-9
First Edition

Copyright © Kelvin Corcoran, 2010.

The right of Kelvin Corcoran to be identified as the author
of this work has been asserted by him in accordance with the
Copyrights, Designs and Patents Act of 1988.
All rights reserved.

Cover design by Peter Hughes.
Image copyright © Peter Hughes, 2010.

Acknowledgements
With thanks to those involved some of these poems have appeared in earlier versions in the following publications:
Angel Exhaust; Fulcrum: An Annual of Poetry and Aesthetics; 10th Muse; Shearsman; Skald; Tremblestone; The Canting Academy; Ahadada; Eyewear; PFS Post.

The first part of 'On the Xenophone Label' appeared as *Xenophanes of Colophon* published by West House Books. 'On the Xenophone Label', 'Madeleine's Letter to Bunting' and 'Learning to Play the Harp' were published in earlier versions by Longbarrow Press.
Thanks to Alan Halsey and Brian Lewis.

Earlier versions of parts of 'From the Hen-Roost' were published in *What Hit Them* by Oystercatcher Press. Some of the longer poems in 'Sing Campion Song' were first written in an abandoned collaboration with Peter Hughes.

I've also recast two earlier poems from *Backward Turning Sea*, and put them to use here as the starting points of the subsequent pieces.

Contents

From Where Song Comes or Keeping the Empire in Order
    From Where Song Comes   11
    Sing Campion Song   15
    Reading *The Cantos*   23
    From the Hen-Roost   30
    A Thesis on the Ballad   34
    Learning to Play the Harp   37

News of Aristomenes   39

The Family Carnival
    Apokriatika   61
    A Season Below Ground   64
    Hearing Mishearing Doug Oliver   66
    Byron's Karagiozis   69
    Epicurus Is My Neighbour   74
    Madeleine's Letter to Bunting   78

On the Xenophone Label   83

Notes   104

"These centuries of the decline of ancient phiolosophy
　Almost forgotten"
　　　　　—John Hall

From Where Song Comes or Keeping the Empire in Order

From Where Song Comes

Descended from tribes of the Tarim Valley,
lost in town, open mouthed at the end of
someone else's tether, heads back, arms up,
offering music for money—some hope.

Eyes flicker like English trees in the park,
picture a scheme planted for self improvement
or maps where the houses and circuits will be,
bloody generations scouring the veins.

A chorus of phonemes, not even ghosts,
we stand disjoint, signatures broken
drilling holes in work, family, the whole lot;
those first words cling like a jacket of smoke.

'Woman', 'arm', 'speak', 'weep', 'hit', 'stone'
differing in fundamental forms, thick with roots,
sound unintelligible, shut out—you were shouting
I didn't understand, doors banging in the street.

If we sing our belonging and away,
listen to the neighbour's rising call;
the song's never the same twice,
if we sing belonging and away.

⋆

There was a moment, perhaps as polyphonic flocks rose from the dark edge of the forest at dawn, an impelling code fills the sky, a code that previously didn't exist when things were themselves.

The village empties, even the dogs leave. This could be in east Sumatra, the Saami steppes, anywhere unrecorded. The hunter-gatherers stand like stone on the green path which has just become unfamiliar. Terror.

A conspiracy foisted on them from the wet earth itself had them invent the seasons. They take their place in the telekinetic supply chains and the plough sings it, the long slow lines in classical tropes of ridge and furrow.

*

Key terms were dropped along the route
polished and ardent, the sun boiling lowered
into the dreamed sea of lyric voices.

Out of the secret meadow and heap of poet's bones
as if in the tradition of the music of the drowned,
they step forward to sing, we know their names.

In the earthquake zones, they speak lightly,
elaborate buried contours and the lost harmonics of
the green shore, the risen mountain, the first house.

How soft was the air when you laid word by word,
is that you girl leaping from the world's edge
hair spread like a dark net to catch the little poets?

In that massively blue and absolute idiom
another life surges after impact, out there
mid-ocean waves, banks of weeds, dark harbour.

*

The words remain part of a composite unit. They may even ignite a fire in the theatre of the fields and sky as framework of the ritual. Some groups did not attain intelligible song but prayed repeatedly. Such as: 'Spear spear strike home,' or 'Father father give me game to kill.'

We can be certain that choral song followed, everyone in the group singing one thought. Archaic survivals are a different matter, waiting in the shadows by the rude door, at the ragged limit of the worked land, buried, and belonging to others unnamed.

And then that moment arrives, the world tilts and everything is
changed. They dug shallow trenches in various scandalous patterns and
filled them with honey and other animal products. He said—the words
come of themselves, shoot up of themselves, a song.

⋆

According to our notions Orpheus has returned from
Egypt melancholic and is teaching weasels to dance;
chant the empty road, the muddy field,
chant Spring cocked in the buried dead
and the dubious benefits of the last revolution.

The behaviour of animals and men is hardly distinct,
the finer points of conduct lost in darkness;
from the garden and the secrets of the house
syllables as emotive sounds take shape,
drowned in the ground plan of abandoned towns.

On the shores of the glittering, frozen sea
they suffer a savage and wretchedly poor life;
feed on wild plants, wear skins, sleep on the ground,
we're at the end of the known world
everything beyond is in the realm of fable.

⋆

What the world needs now is a theory of song,
a thesis on the ballad to free the words in our mouths;
there will be songs for dancing round, songs for sleep,
a song for helping a person across a river.

From the licensed street corner, a version of a version
from another country rings out many voices in one,
songs for masked dancers, performed for the girls
songs of the laws of the school, kneeling on the ground.

Let it unruin many a poor boy, standing next to the gap
an oasis or total knowledge maxed in the echo chamber,
and work songs for Spring, for weeding, planting and rain,
a song of gifts of beer, for wife takers and wife givers.

Boys dancing with reed-pipes, girls with drums,
the other time we enter now is everything.

Sing Campion Song

Today the trees are massive and the air in limbo
makes me think of those working hard to keep me in sunglasses,
to keep me in song,—it's worth it to send me gliding along the streets,
through the flushed and coloured map of unending desire.

Thomas Campion is my neighbour, he lives on the top floor,
he breathes the pure counter-tenor ozone from the tower of song;
though the civic society wanted him out, he's not coming down,
he tells them to drop it and sings louder every night.

But imagine a common purpose in breathing the next breath
and the blossom bursts so candid, like love unfolding,
like a river of untethered clouds naming a new country,
to make us unsay each hectic word in the artless plan.

Sing Campion song eyes closed
this ayre is not recorded on a mail base
leaning onto the edge of darkness
step out where comfort is she will.

*

Campion's perfect iambics oh
what can we do what can
equal the lute river melody
of English poetry beginning.

*

Their boat sailed up the Thames
wood oud Italian loot to her
making fowre parts in counter-point
that they might move stone by sound.

*

My Campion is singing
in the mountain grove
3 for 2 and petrol rush
the wanton country made.

If we talk like this I don't know that I get it,
impasto Sam in the Darent valley, the boys at leapfrog,
error message 208 sings in the forest of night
and the precipitation trailing westward peters out.

At some point for the locals it must tilt,
and where shall we find our colours then?
The forgotten use of realgar, the decline of arsenic,
will you make me a white to match this radiance?

After the abandonment found on lyric stairways
the theory of craft labour took hold in Cambridge,
the Sunni triangle of old learning and money;
London das kapital of foreign occupation.

If songs make us free, we already have them all,
called conflict of interest in the history of the English jig.

*

White van man morning
paths in the sky announce
Campion Restoration
a cure for pain antique.

        *

Flicker of Solanum trails clouds
as if by one voyce to an INSTRUMENT
the robin's erratic flight path tells you
there is ever one fresh spring.

        *

At the back of the house the green
shaft releases a day from
the box of song all around us
from holes in the lid the light beams.

        *

Campion in two three and
foure parts radio nowhere
glory intermittent fills the air
burning down the house.

They say he can explain music, that's the way,
whisper in our bones ape heartbeat, I like it,
guarding the gate at night against
running around the poorer quarters
or the sea's endless sifting of the land
so that our children might sing in the vetch and lettuce.

They say he can explain the ship that left us here,
dark imprint at the western edge, disappeared,
to rise as factories plotted across the fields,
a history of betrayal, a history of anything other than
—this is what I do now and the rest will fit,
coasting the unknown world at first light
my girls laughing in the empty chambers of air,
a herring gull cry linotypes the sea.

    *

Tuned to the moving spheres
Apollo made village music visible
dot dash radar narrates the sky
our migrant route unearthed.

*

There's a face in the garden
a ghost in the house   forensic trace
of the lost songs of Astraea
a red oh on her ripe mouth.

*

Winter on the stave rattles
the window winter on the stave
shakes the rowan sheds light
raising the house acoustic.

*

O Campion swallow your fate
unlock the logic table submit
dark ravisher the chiefe beginner
may well be soong.

This may well be what's called outside.
Are you going outside? From outside you can see
the massive walls built to guard the capital,
the capital and its monopolistic discourse;
various birds fly into it, their brains, dunk dunk,
another brace, a bag of feathers hits the deck.

We set out over snowfields in glacial air,
there's music sounding underground
magnetism conspires in black soil furrows,
the rise and fall of it, as if all our lives we're leaving
and the place was not even here a generation ago,
now there's no telling, the telegram stations unimaginable.

It's not that you're some traveller in a strange land,
it's not that you'll log the days after occupation;
but your tracks inscribe a name not yours
and the sound hangs in the chambered air
—what invention it took to shape one song,
and how the children's voices flood the trees.

```
C  A  M  P  I  O  N
A  S  T  R  A  E  A
M  U  S  I  C  K  E
P  U  R  S  U  E  S
I  A  M  B  I  C  S
O  R  D  A  I  N  E
N  A  T  I  O  N  S
```

Reading *The Cantos*

1

Fell asleep in the courtyard reading *The Cantos*
after swimming rolled on white waves and ankle stones,
Malatesta and the Magnificent, the bloody mechanics.

After the dazzling verse and magnetic names
I remembered two hours sat before the girl Aphrodite,
the intermittent light and the crowd parting occasionally.

Her hair lifts, she dreams the name of a new world,
the sea surrounds us on all sides and the light
comes and goes over her meadows and pathways.

What does Pound find to admire in Sigismundo and the Medici?
Hands grasping the rods of power, banking and patronage,
polishing the azure air for the faces of Tuscan gods?

I woke up in cherry season, ate the cherries ripe and wet,
the sea breathing in the olive groves, clouds rising from the hills,
to see ants hoist crumbs to a depthless sky.

*

The wind cases the house all night
rolls away to reveal the harbour washed
the sea lanes rise and fall.

How grand to propound the big idea;
interest rates as rented money
made all art go rotten after 1527.

A species of modernist ambition
to synthesise the culture's cache,
a gesture, anti-Semitic and parochial.

The wind cases the house at night
to reveal the coastline hung out to dry,
Europe and the Faithful heard on the air.

Chanting of dumb beasts sanctioned
their reasoning is shallow
they speak to popular prejudice.

Small birds drill the sky in an agony
of Spring it is it is it is the force of them,
they sing song a theology of awake.

The merchants of the Morea carried
the sprouting branch and sharp mind
where she sets her foot to the sea.

What nerve they had to outstare
Methoni and Corroni, eyes of
the serene empire's trade routes.

Platsa, above us on the mountain, traded
directly with Venice on donkeys, down
the calderimi to the harbour of the world.

*

And then in Canto XLIX his genius
breaks your heart, imperial power is
what is it?—the rushing particles ignite.

The little owl glides to its shadow
high on the wall of the broken tower
above the middle sea that makes us.

The widow walks across the square
she is not long a widow, she is a black line
carrying road-side flowers to her neighbour.

Turning the dynamo Cadmus turned
Euratos rises on the running wave
Europa of wide open eyes steps ashore.

Everywhere
          scattered song
the host
      a fishing boat draws the west skyline

2

In Pisa at night the wind rattles the gate of the cage and fingers a poet's bones.

In Pisa at night he dreamt hypostasis, he dreamt he understood the poor and sided with monsters.

In Pisa at night the modernist preference for antiquity over the present was stuffed and hung upside down from a lamp-post.

In Pisa at night hell in a black wave rolled off the Tuscan hills drowning the terraces of Dioce—learn to fear your own stupidity, the wind rising in your face barking bad economics.

In Pisa at night our beautiful singer broken, his mouth removed, his thinking fills the death cell.

              *

Last night with a half moon risen
we watched the fires across the gulf
reduced to five points of yellow light
Corroni burning, the sea dark and still.

A silver jackal started from the undergrowth
quick paws running in the dust

and we felt the weight of him
sounding on the hollow ground.

*

In the stacked heat of noon
the sparrows will only come down
in the narrow shade of the bent tree
to bathe in the dust bowl stubble.

Later the wind circles the square
making a conference of the trees
the eucalyptus to the olive to the pine
sounding notes one to another Aeolian.

*

Moon, cloud, tower—here Christeas's tower stands against the sea
to protect the harbour from pirates and other crude usurers or, where,
after robbing their neighbours, the Christeas hid, and they're here still.

Morritt in 1795 speaks of the splendid generosity of the Captain,
a picnic set out in the long hall of entertainment and on the green
around the tower, a hundred guests enjoy the hospitality of the Boss.

Pound is out there, battering on history, raging in the square,
the fluty music of various birds on various wires indifferent;
Musso, Confucius, Odysseus swap places in his empty mouth.

Pound's out there, gone ape in the Broken Ant-Hill Book of Reference;
let them run through the groves at night over smashed marble,
let their music saunter from a distant village on the scaled air.

You could sit still in a village abandoned under waves of summer,
just look at things—people and animals and trees tell you everything;
moon over cloud over tower and the owls making sweet kills.

Know that if you sail south from here the first island you find is Cythera:
Come Aphrodite, our lady of honey and liquefied limbs,
Come seafoam girl, come out to us on calm water and in storm.

*

Peter, an unexpected mildness came over me this late afternoon at
Yannis's taverna. The sea rolled in and out, I drank a Mythos and half
recognized Márta Sebestyén singing a version of Deep Forest.

This was after a night of shortwave rant, belief burning in every language
of the world like a tight band around the neck. You hear it coming
through, 'the low percentage of reason which seems to operate in human
affairs.' It makes uncertainty a gift. And tonight on Radio Rome . . .

*

Rain fell this afternoon, mid-August rain, rare,
afterwards the earth came up smelling spicy
at the bedroom window, rain for the Panagiya.

We make a party for God's mother,
lights strung across the harbour, ribbons of light
and tonight pork and rice and beer.

Also for the fishing men Christeas,
amplified music late into the soft night
with fireworks, flares and guns.

Boats tied up:
> Alexandra
> Veloz
> Maria
> Alexandros
> Argonautis
> There's no boat called Coded History.

*

Vatic recital of bank rates does not
make for the revealed truth of history;
this ideogram means overbearing insistence
about a pile of broken sticks
does not make a tree.

There is no argument.

No boat called Coded History floats.

The temple is not for sale,
let the old man at the gate rest
you can pay when you leave;
the grass sways, his mind swings
asleep awake fitful magpie.

This green pot has outdone
your arrogance   out of it
from 3,000 years ago a smell
orange blossom honey
and the freedom of doubt.

*

(drafts and fragments)

the slight Mediterranean tide paints
the rocks a pale margin between worlds

kids squealing dive bomb off the harbour wall
there's a snake in the water trough to bite your feet

and the waves lazy flop reaches afternoon
translating blue green water and light

Ezra Pound is rolling rocks down the mountain
at the edge of the European mind, rubble, empires of rubble

the empty house where the sky spreads
stands in the dry river bed abandoned

saved by foxes and cicadas
                                  their parliament

From the Hen-Roost

'War, one war after another, men start 'em who couldn't put up a good hen-roost.'

1

Black ships drawn up for ten years
to get an exquisite woman, to get at all the women.

To master trade routes, grain supplies, pipelines of wealth
burning lights of acquisition scored on the map.

Make a poem of it; a bayful of weapons in the sun
a poem; the fertile plain a killing ground unrolled

Runs in every direction—delight in slaughter found
the great host fell upon Asia's meadowland and marshes.

2

Karl Twitcher out in the field geologises
no water or gold found but thought
there might be oil out here, let's talk.

Philby bows to the father of his new nation
lips wet from Zamzam, sets about God's work
the American concession secured.

Osama sits on the banks of the River Gash,
wives safely stowed in Khartoum,
sings—ain't gonna study war no more.

At the crossroads of Nejd the Word rose up
from the Buner Mountains, the King of the West,
farming abandoned to wire the faith.

Osama dreams of smart women, burning towers
of Qutb by the waters of Manhattan
of an old bitch gone in the teeth.

Every grain of sand becomes a gem,
and Lord—Israel's tents do shine so bright,
Aramco on the tribal mat, afloat in the Gulf.

3

We had thought them easy meat
for jackals, leopards, wolves
but now . . . across the moat on high ground
Trojans reaping.

It came down hard on us
what if we pull out, wait off shore?
the rampart breached, Europe stranded
by the ships, politicians at the old business.

They go licking up the paid, fat words
in a greased circuit of ignorance;
gods in bliss in Houston and Riyadh
granted the power of massacre.

My brothers dropped in to the sleep
of bronze, their accents mapping
the poor cities of an indifferent country,
as they leaked into the ground.

4

Breathing long alcohol afternoons he might tell me about the war,
thick layers of it. The stories thick as beer and rum breath and I still
don't know the truth, the final version. He volunteered himself out of

the Free State and poverty to cross the Irish Sea, the gulf of sad song
misery, for the spit-shine British Army. Out of what? I don't know.

He was shipped out to India and off to fight in Burma with the
forgotten 14th. He went on about the filth, the child prostitutes, just
girls waiting in alleyways with men shouting the prices. Bored, they
would set traps for kites, tie bread with string and allow the birds to
swoop down, swallow the bread and fly off, then yank them out of the
sky and kill them.

They were half buried in jungle tracks, tunnels of festering vegetation
without names, and the stacked humidity just makes you rot—and
then, Jesus, the bloody insects at you, at you, all the time—and on top
of that the Jap bastards trying to fucking shoot you for free.

And if men like him had not gone to it?

I don't know what they made of their fear; dark bird hovering there
for years, just out of vision, ready to slide off the air, dive and tear
and shred; one of Chadwick's beasts would do, sharp eyed, clawed.
Armitage could identify the model; outline its shape, as it ghosts in and
out of the mind for decades.

5

And Thatcher's nasty little war
and Blair's nasty rented wars,
at some point they believe
then retire to revelation on the Red Sea.

We hear their voices like ghosts on the air,
the false tone burning, smeared on a nation.

May their houses be drowned in black dust.
May their words be as waves of dead locusts.
May their fake empire be struck dumb.
And may the names of the dead be made real to them.

6

The bay empties itself, the deep-sea ships sail away
Homer doesn't cover this, if he did I would rewrite it.

The boy looked out to sea, it was empty, he was astonished
—nothing on the radar, just static, just radiation ghosts.

Peace like a white vision, bees murmur in the marram,
and light paints the surface of the whole world.

Somewhere, ships low on the water, take cover,
their discrete weaponry a design feature.

Somewhere, rewritten—speedboats take a punt at the Cole,
Odysseus already dreams of Ithaka pitching under his feet.

And the elemental gods flatten the rampart
as if nothing ever happened here.

A Thesis on the Ballad

Barbara Allen

Are you singing from that other place unbearable
though you would not have the girl
look away in Scarlet Town with her killer beauty.

From that room when I was young
I saw the light lie low under a sky of blue hills
after the houses where I walked but was blind.

I think this song may be locked in the brain
even at death, it sounds out as cells close
—Oh Barbara Allen what have you done to me.

An Expanse of Water

The water is wide I can't get o'er
possessed at every stroke the great
aching distance between us
across which I would row, swim or ski.

If the waves break in common measure
fish in the sea you know how I feel
when she walked to the water lay down
and spoke her underwater words to me.

The Truth

'The Seven Sisters was a true song. It happened back yonder in Mutton Hollow. I was there myself. Somebody got killed over the girl. I was there soon after it happened.'

Psychopaths

Edward and Lord Randall want nothing from you
your part is to fall into the ditch of absent motive
evil and misery exist: you cannot rhyme them out.

Edward and Lord Randall want nothing from you
the greenwood mulch is stuffed rich with corpses
my love lies unalone beneath the sweet birdy trees.

Edward, Lord Randall and the Demon Lover
run in the blood at the singing edge of the world
and you will never win those shining hills again.

Class War and Sex War

We shall all be made to pay one day
lying on the snowy bed of silk
to fiddle music in the wood unceasing.

Red and grinning Little Musgrave returns
arm in arm with Lamkin, a blood-dark night
away boys away to Ireland and the Hebrides.

To the roots of narrative in rock, ice and fire
before the saga of riches crashed
where the mind might lodge at zero.

Out of a shining sea of its own telling
we shall all be made to pay one day
hear the dogs bark and the footfall at the door.

And So

If anyone should ask you
do you know who wrote this song?
It was I and I sing it all day long.

It came from the dark dark earth
and all those lives of beasts and men
go doubling in the wood at night.

Those figures still unstill
ford the black river rolling
and the vocal bird calls—here here here.

Learning to Play the Harp

The lost poems of W.S. Graham written
as a boy in Govan and in all of his life,
the shipyard night-shift listens still
to John McCormack on Radio Éire sing
The Harp That Once at closedown.

Silent now, night tenor of silence
shed on the dark waters of the Clyde,
as if words might launch the boy across
the black river, another world, no more
at closedown and dawn, they're gone, as the smoke.

*

Have you ever heard anything as sweet as that?
though Sydney's radio was not bought at Spicer's shop.

And that would be my dad around the house somewhere
singing the same song, he drones in and out of the tune.

It was all taken from us you know, by the English, the war
of loss and burnt letters, the despised and disappearing past.

His voice steps in and out of the tune, up the stairs
making still the house, the garden in deeper silence.

Fixing the boy in place counting down he sees
the grain in the black wooden chair deepen.

The anti-Orpheus, darkness spilling from his hands,
pity the man in the alcohol box: you can do nothing.

*

Of course it was the morning
up early for apprenticeship

when the radio played the harp
before the train to Glasgow.

My good mistake at first light
to sing the song I didn't know,
the boy dreamt the night before
the poem unwritten in the shipyard.

Andrew—your term, migrating
over the border and awa' for
Scotland and the Duncan generation,
the savage survival flight path.

Turning back on itself, the past
a brown river running through town,
invisible the dead crowd the banks
made quiet under a ribbon of mist.

I remembered walking home
in the early hours thinking of her,
her mouth made me dumb
—will you come across the water to me.

The moon sat on the top of a hedge
at the end of her dad's garden,
half the night we lay there
her face in victory in a square of light.

Of course that was the morning
walking by the closed shops,
the river is green not brown
and above the weir it widens.

It speaks and slips its rhythm,
and I launch the One Hope off the map
from the mud and flattened reeds,
the sky wheeling and released.

NEWS OF ARISTOMENES

'. . . and the gods would be kinder to them because they were defending their own and not committing a first injustice.'

—Yanni, what do you know about Aristomenes?
—Hmm, not too much . . . we could Google it.

1

I am Aristomenes of Andania and I will tell you everything,
what I did and did not do, how I invented the moment of decisive action,
the birth of fear which clears a field of men, Messenia of Laconians
—that was the history of the second rebellion.

What in the world would make me leave my village?
The buzz of bees, my olives fattening like black jewels,
the wagtail patrolling my patch in familiar light,
though the wind plays naughty in the Stenyklaros Valley.

It's true I refused the title of king, I accepted Captain,
I keep close to the men and their leaders, keep them even closer to me;
I can spot the traitors and be magnanimous, for others to deal with
and roll them in a ditch for pigs to snout out and feast on.

It's also true I ran once, from those bastard godly twins,
that doubling of them, against one mortality, defeats me;
I ran, I lost my shield, they may have been in a tree, or hovering
in my mind all along, in an empty sky, dread undid me.

They hail me three times Hekatomphonia—well, so it is then,
I am spattered in their red words up to my elbows;
a fox at the chickens makes feathers fly, and a little blood travels far
—of course a fox can slink out of the mouth of hell and look smart.

It's true I stole into their capital and laid tribute to Athena,
I danced into their heart, the brazen chamber, how flashy, how dazzling;
I laced their gruel with panic that morning, the streets trembled:
war's in the mind, I invaded theirs, my mouth's a weapon.

The stories of my charmed escape from capture are all true,
the stories of my escape from death are all from my mouth.
Think, no man returns from below ground. Have you talked to him?
Shared a drink? Held his hand and felt its warmth? No, I think not.

Yes I did consult the oracles, sources of power I plugged into;
the making of a secondary meaning has a single edge: action.
The dark contract, unseen, unspoken, of the earth, I know what I want,
you know the names of my victories and they will not be forgotten.

As for the mysteries, like a snake even nonsense bites, mock as you might;
the matter of my birth is secret, what I buried on Mount Ithome is not,
who knows what happens if you sleep in the narcotic shade of the fig?
the old goddess may rise a girl, trees thicken, the stream run fresh.

From the beginning there have always been stories about me,
I uphold the oracles of Lykos and I will recover Messenia;
my watchers are out on the hills and I'm ready,
I am Aristomenes of Andania and I will tell you everything.

2

In the bar opposite the Blue Café
from the heart of mechanical song
why not why not why not take time out,
this is what comes of beating pretty on a log.

There's a kiosk and a prize grab cabinet,
you can win a pink dolphin, a bear, a gold watch,
you can see the sea through a glass cube, the sea dancing,
where we parade sunlit after the earthquake.

Off Navarinou the Ottoman fleet goes down,
Gregory Peck steps up—don't argue with fire power,
in town three pyramidal wedding dresses in a row
prepare to go ballistic, lick of smoke whispers 3 2 1.

Finally on Shoe Street, the oral tradition is fixed,
SOUTH EMPIRE rises a line of fortified cities,
a realignment of the world, we have photographic proof,
ends in a fault running down Aristomenes.

*

According to Herodotus Aristagoras said to the Spartans—the Messenians have no gold or silver, or anything worth fighting for. So why should you bother fighting them? Go get the Persians. The Spartans did not listen and Aristomenes stepped forward.

*

We stayed two nights in the Hakos Hotel, Kalamata. It's on the seafront, scene of the allied rout in World War 2. As the Nazis bombed and strafed the crowded beaches the sea ran red with the blood of British and Commonwealth troops. They headed down into the Mani for evacuation to Crete. In the small harbours the dilapidated ships were bombed repeatedly and, although not hit, collapsed from the vibrations in the water.

We watched a film in the Hakos Hotel. Bruce Willis set out to rescue some good Africans from some bad Africans. There was talk of mineral rivalry. In fact Bruce's mission was to helicopter out a white doctor, she was French but with American citizenship. Bloodied Bruce, heroic maverick, went against orders; he wasn't meant to save non-Americans at all. The advert break on Greek TV is long and I was able to go down five floors, buy beer at the kiosk and return before Bruce resumed bleeding and rescuing liberally.

⋆

To test the endurance of the oral tradition and the life of myth I was thinking what to ask in Andania, where Aristomenes may have been born perhaps 2,600 years ago. 'Messene: A Dream Come True' by Eva Maria Leng and Waltraud Sperlich speaks of the Messenians as a people seeking and dreaming a homeland, drawing parallels to migrant workers in contemporary Europe. It espouses romance, destiny and ecology with the unsuppressed mood music of the great homecoming. I think it must be written for idiots, tipped that way. The 3D postcard of Delphi is more useful. The picture has a fine corrugated surface, like a mechanical sea in regulated waves. Tilt it one way the ruin of the site is seen, then at another angle the theatre is restored and time dismissed; an illusion printed in ridges. Remember Pausanias—'These are the stories; believe one or another according to which side you want to be on.'

⋆

In Messene the stone base for a bronze statue was discovered built into the wall of the apse of the basilica. The inscription is **ΑΡΙΣΤΟΜΕΝΗΣ** By the 4th century A.D. the city was abandoned, ruined by the collapse of Rome, earthquakes and barbarian raids.

⋆

And then a morning so fresh
like a massive wet diamond
suspended above the white sea

with the tatty mimosa blowing and
the container ships stuck on the water
we went off around Taygetos
tottering and twisting in the air.

*

Mount Ithome folds itself around Messene,
layered blue hills, undulant olive trees white and green
roll out beyond sight to the plain and Spartan wall;
the city a natural amphitheatre, Hippodamian and mighty.

In founding Messene, above all they sought Aristomenes,
invoked and asked to return and dwell with them;
hillside rubble and scrub, bare earthworks, postholes,
roots turned over, the light invades every mote.

All the birds of Mavrommati sing and gentle rain rains down,
music falling in a green chamber for the river god of Pamisos;
from good red soil, over buried pillars, anenomies, hyacinths, daisies,
Oh Artemis on a bed of vetch most purple.

Later Melanie said—that flower we saw everywhere
that was mallow, sort of mauve, just everywhere;
and above all, at this point in the poem, I wanted to tell you
exactly what was there, unintoxicated, in April, recovering.

3

The best of it was our night raiding with the Fox,
blood released runs like black soup in that pitch;
with his rage on him he was a sight to behold
but once you looked there was no unseeing then.

It was a sort of sacrifice gone wrong, like butchery
the soft plopping of purple organs, knotty innards
by way of knife and spike onto our innocent soil,
eviscerate steam rising like a shitty ghost.

Hekatomphonia means we always counted the dead,
if you don't count the dead the dead don't count,
like in the kingdom of the two rivers, remote slaughter
remains on the eye and a terrible blindness is born.

We would slip out of Ithome into the arms of darkness
and everything smelt good, the fields in perfumed waves;
we were like kids rolling around a herb garden,
rags wrapped around our blades for silence ungleaming.

They would stand in dumb rows at a stockade—ripe for slitting,
or we'd catch a troop in a narrow pass and open the last gate for them.

*

He certainly did steal into Sparta one night, disguised,
right into the temple of Athena, bronze chamber, keeper of the city,
and laid his shield in tribute, as if from another world;
as intended, terror fell on the Laconians, like a knife to the bone.

He came trotting back after the mischief that morning and told us;
he had a charming tongue and could undo ropes and women with it,
you might ask Archidameia about this, devotee of Demeter etc,
she released him, covered her tracks and off he went like a boy in Spring.

You could also ask that farmer's daughter, she dreamt of him
and he turns up captive to a gang of Cretan archers, and again
the woman sets him free, and off he went driving out Laconians;
we wrecked their markets and made riot, whole areas abandoned.

He was chief kidnapper, cattle raider, three times hekatomphonia,
we sang that streets would be named after him, in Pherae say;
he knew the meaning of action like a distinct language,
he was the tin-sheet Andanian mystery boy and, as it goes, our saviour.

When it was all up he did the right thing by us, our captain;
we went into dread exile, some place—Zancle, Sicily—to the west.

          ★

They would have us kill for words but you can take the story
as you see fit; whether the fool floated down borne by an eagle
or his shield let him bounce like a little lamb is unimportant;
the point is he returned and killed lots of Laconians.

They say there was something strange about him from birth,
he was favoured, his mother slept with a god in the likeness of a snake;
well that's pretty special—no wonder there were stories about him,
they talk and talk and he did all those things.

If he walked into town everyone downed tools, ribbons and flowers
      would fly,
the women would start singing impromptu, raising the dust and the rest;
he fought at all those places, Boar's Grave, Great Trench and led us out
      of siege,
we weren't serfs then, backs bent in the fields for another's tragedy.

That winter snow sat on the mountains all around us, a white bowl;
the river beds flooded and froze and old ones died by thin fires,
shadows of clouds like bunched black fists fell on the hills again and again;
he led us out of siege, in a spear shaped column we tore through Laconians.

I know another thing too—at the end of defeat he went to Rhodes;
he was old, he thought of Sardis, of Ekbatana, and died.

4

Aristomenes hunted Laconians on the plain and high mountain
Aristomenes went into Sparta at night, left Spartan spoil in Sparta's heart
Aristomenes laid his shield in the bronze house temple for Athena
Aristomenes went into Argos and Arcadia, allies and exiles returned
Aristomenes charmed Demeter's priestesses and escaped to Ithome
Aristomenes believed in the execution of memorable action and terrorising
      Laconians
Aristomenes fought at the Boar's Grave at the Great Trench and escaped
Aristomenes and his 300 stole corn, cattle and wine and drove the enemy out

         ★

When the Spartans came over the mountain
and made us their slaves,
self appointed lords of the way it is
with their global credit, pipelines
and smart weapons in phalanx,
our irrelevance came to an end.

The hills at a certain hour turned mauve
and these men emerged in our fields
as if out of nowhere, clouds around their thighs,
their mouths barking—Helot—Barbarian—Outdweller;
they made Leuctra into an arms dump
and the crypteia proved themselves at night.

We had invented six languages in the dust,
mastered the olive, grape and grain
and tied the knots in an epic poetry;
on discs of light dropped by the gods
we walked the broken path of the sea
and still knew the songs the birds sang.

Your picture of the world can be undone,
stations off the air, iron ore shipped out;

the sky as blue, the terraces of the sea rise and fall
enough to break your heart each morning;
we no longer walked the ground,
the earth a shadow for another's empire.

*

Aristomenes has been thrown into deep Keadas and left for dead
Aristomenes has floated to the floor of the chasm on an eagle's spread wings
Aristomenes glides in the bronze light of the eagle on his shield
Aristomenes has drawn his cloak over his head and is waiting to die
Aristomenes has woken up to see a vixen nosing at corpses
Aristomenes has followed the vixen out of the shadows step by step
Aristomenes has been dragged by the clever one to the light and to Eira
Aristomenes went down into death and came back after three days to Eira

5

Aristomenes buried [the thing?] on Mount Ithome
[   ] what   [it . . . .] was   [was]

Andanian   [   ]
[unknown] tin sheet – mystery   stamp[ed]

brazen chamber, bronze jar and [inside]
beaten to fineness [there was] a scroll

rescue [   ] old woman, you see
inscribed   goddess   the Great [one]

from her [hands]   instructions
[after death]   how   [to live]

               *

(To do the right thing even in defeat
Aristomenes buried the thing on Mount Ithome,
defeat as inevitable as the wild fig
bending to the stream or an oracular pun.)

               *

Cities buried, walls gone under meadows
olive groves over sanctuaries

they talk and talk
and the mountain grows

Meligala—on the upper or northern Messenian plain
—honeymilk

In Pig Valley, thick with trees, dark all day
—a sanctuary of Artemis

the names: marrow in the white bones.

> *

Aristomenes buried the thing on Mount Ithome
Epaminondas dug it up after centuries
drew a circle on the ground, drew in streets and walls

> *

Messenians absent for 300 years

did not change their customs
nor lose their Dorian dialect

rain-broken, thunder-broken
the white bones

> *

And they went to Zancle, Sicily
the west darkening, the record dim

> short is the way
> and our Lady golden
> long is the way
> and our Lady golden

the Greeks there sing songs of the xenitia
of living away, to the north, to the factories

from 800 BC in Salento, Calabria and Sicily
Doric still spoken from a 6,000 word lexicon

Doric spoken valley to valley
villagers untouched by writing

    Oh my beautiful Morea
    I will not see you again
    I have my father my mother my brother
    all buried in the earth here
    I will not see you again

old woman climbing steps
   the Great One   a girl
from her hands the song
   our Lady golden

     ★

In Andania the tattered banners proclaim
the perpetual season teased by the wind, a dog,
it could be new year—may you have many years.

The dog tears another strip and it could be
Easter for the god risen indeed
or No Day for victorious defeat.

Time sits by the road smoking
 the bus is late and there's no post,
Aristomenes sits by the road breaking empires.

6

I sit in the shade of this fig-tree
and wait and watch in the still air

washed from the backward turning sea
blue mountains fade in the haze

moment by moment the many words for light
rise, enough to hide a whole country

she laid the path over rock over water
everything I did she held in her hands

they will return from there
eyes gone dark with seeing

nearby a woodpigeon calls and
small birds sing in a chamber of sound

chirrup nations of chaos chirrup
a message draining the secret meadows

but slowly through the afternoon
the bronze bowl of silence fills

over there they are building
after fire and earthquake and war

tap tapping away for hope
shaping stone time will pock

*

The fact white hot and near silent
in the squares and streets of Eira,
burning like a chamber of fire or forge
for making swords, proving men.

At the heart of it Sparta,
can only make itself in other lands
can only enslave, stamping Sparta
on strangers' faces in rows.

At the heart of it system collapse,
weapons technique, hidden deals,
the abduction of women and
cattle raiding dreamed night-long.

Fire makes a mirage of walls and towers
the sea sounding in a tunnel of
turning air, those voices high in Taygetos
fall upon us to map the risen world.

⁕

With morning coming over the roof
shadow falls on shadow to disappear,
something has driven the world into this
dark pilot of the course taken.

Self-appointed arbiters squeak by rote
—if it is fragmented, inchoate, so it must be written:
baleful Anacreon, get out of it,
go learn the song again.

Light steps over the roof, shadow on shadow,
war reports shake the air, wave after wave
piling up women and children in mounds;
this is what we do, only the names change.

We didn't stop from raising Messenia
lest Spartans took exception;
we hit hard, employed art, watched the hills
waited their approach—and for what?

The tangle of branches on the wall
a language, trace its slow progress;
the cicadas dry music its signature,
day advances, all meaning's changed.

*

What I do is sit under the fig-tree and wait
at the point of death everything comes to life,
time stops and then whips, on the crumbling edge
of Keadas, birds wheeling below.

It might be a gentle wind lifts your sleeve
fresh as my love's breath, the light shows through
each fibrous thread, like wings extended
and their hands on your shoulders push.

The unimaginable darkness breaks out then,
in the pine trees bending and scattered rocks
whiteness pushing up through scrub,
rats, jackals, birds and frogs swoon to earth in a rush.

As in battle, it breaks out, blood leaking
from a young face, close up, the black hair soaked,
it all snaps shut, silence, and then the roar exalting,
a town goes up in smoke, a gleaming pile of spoil.

I sit, I wait, they keep the noise down around me,
dust falls in dark rooms, the sea nearby translates time;
smiling physicians appear through the curtains,
I expect a song and dance routine of sorts.

*

She sings in the morning in and out of the kitchen
as birds sing because the sun rises
saying I was awake late last night,
her mouth opening and closing in yellow light.

I've returned several times from where there is no singing,
from Keadas, from Trophonius and at Leuctra, to Spartan frenzy;
they will call me exegete of the katabasis, or some such,
and each time there was never a girl singing like this one.

You have to go there and strike a dark bargain,
lie down, hold barley cakes mixed with honey,
go feet first into a mouth in the earth and shoot away
as if caught in a river, a river of blackness covers your head.

The return is difficult and never the same route as the descent,
I scratched a few words in seeds and blood on the passing rock;
she laces the air with her singing, there's a lucky boy in the village
and bees drift through clouds of flour as she claps and claps.

Coda

Even before Lycurgus launched Year Zero
and exported familial sadism as empire
everything unfolds in the high meadows
of the Hellenic subduction zone, its music
travelling westward at 3.5 mm per year.

Leonidas' palace is a casino of vanilla and gold,
the taxis of Sparta are red with white roofs
and snow shines its April message from Taygetos,
against the wall of that wall the sea a bloody memory
of Aristomenes sword dancing on the other side.

The language of action has dropped us here,
the forces of Anatolia, Africa and Eurasia
converge, grind and slide under our feet,
if the roaring speaks another poetry
a head lifts up pouring roots and red soil.

The Family Carnival

Apokriatika

Driving across to the Mani this February we broke the journey in Corinth. Slept the night in a stone cold room in the Hotel Shadow and ate at the taverna used by the villagers for a night out. We thought nothing of the children dressed in Pierrot costumes and Disney. Later I thought I saw a goat faced man outside the door in pitch darkness wearing a white veil, I thought his friend was wearing a Dolly Parton-style wig.

Next morning we drove on and saw big red and green kites on sale everywhere. Men standing and talking at the *kafeneio* were dressed in ball gowns and wigs. Well, village life we thought, you make your own entertainment. We found out the next day it was carnival—Apokriatika, the last weekend before Clean Monday of only fish and vegetables, but for now pre-lenten celebrations held sway. I remembered the carnival songs; cocks and cunts dancing around fruit trees, young boys being taken in hand by aunty at the mill and black straw faced devils chasing through the streets.

*

From the Hotel Shadow on the edge of spring
under the lit rock of Acro Corinth
flash of white wing on the black window,
figures waiting by the door to the world.

Surrounded by the sweep of orange groves
painted booths line the sacred way,
women on their knees whispering Aphrodite
stirring a dark perfume in the deep green leaves.

From Hotel Shadow on the edge of spring
the utilitarian stables of Euro business
fall away to the gulf of crowded boats,
transporting televisions, cars and kitchens.

The lower world cracks apart on successive days
and we open casks, cups and pots in turn,
I think this is before the church, for Dionysus—yes yes,
Dionysus in flight from winter making us mad.

*

The earth cracks in season
and memory set aside rises
by generation, vivid, unchanged.

I think he died in great pain,
drinking aftershave—old spice
and boot polish—on parade.

Are such themes found in folk song?
I don't know. Who is singing?
It's just the nature of the alcoholic.

But I am fifty now and still
I can barely tell you,
here's the last line, I made it.

*

February is the month of the dead
the month of purification

the wine god in his garlands
flirts and slips and stumbles

the earth parting for the eager dead
they come from another country to have their fill

we are not who we seem
we don't sing what you think

*

They lived in a village in another country
my mother would pick out its tunes,
hymns by ear, forgive our foolish ways
—well someone should, and laugh like a girl.

Lead kindly light between the wars,
her father built a business, fruit and veg to market,
all gone in the fatal crash on early morning ice
and the children taken in by relatives.

And before him the journeyman tailor,
a tall, dark man from Slad the narrow valley
and tight mouth, his wife from Bisley,
an even meaner place if possible.

I know them only by her stories
and she's been dead more than twenty years,
they set out across Hardy's fields,
their rough old songs beating in the heart.

*

And dancing uncle is pregnant with a balloon,
he leads his son the satyr with lopsided breasts,
and his daughter, Happiness, skips in circles laughing;
tomorrow is Clean Monday for vegetables and fish.

No—your feet like this, two two, one one, you lead
for Anthesteria, the days of risen ghosts about the city,
let me daub the doors with pitch and chew the buckthorn clean.
Souls—you've had your dish of grain and seeds—now go, now go.

Plastic trumpets and party poppers announce
you can beat Mr Death with a squeaky hammer,
hit him hard and run around the busy tables;
uncle gives birth to a goat, here's the skin to wrap you up in.

Season Below Ground

Melanie this is the motorway we always drove
then and now the fields and towns at rest
falling away in darkness on both sides.

To the west a circuit of lights around a distant hill
rising as if beyond the sea sounds the history
of families made quiet under a spreading sky

Or in that house they might have out lived youth
before all their choirs went under the waves,
face down in the wet garden when time stopped.

It was always this road, up and down the country,
always the blinding cartography in endless parallel
missing the point of where we go.

I think this interior light travels with us,
your face looking forward as the music wanders
the dark enfolding road we leave behind.

*

Arrhythmic mouth opens and wordless speaks
electric buttons random firing, circuit shot
down amongst the dead men, out behind
the dark and dirty, crowded door—Anacreon.

It's about the size of a man flat on the ground,
hidden in the garden, and hardly seals a vacuum now;
we need trees here for the birds to perform from
and there should be consideration of the robin.

Chipping at the window, augorous, aggressive and bonny,
will you do your wings down bury me in mulch
song and dance backward routine to rain black streets?

Take the fires of hell on your breast for us,
slice up winter into strips of transparent sky,
catch light-bearing breath on the sounding screen.

*

When I wrote *The Red and Yellow Book*
events interrupted the writing dream,
a marriage, the mighty book, a death;
a series made indiscrete, bloody and personal.

In that line my own relations gone like smoke,
across the white fields as if from nowhere
my girls turned into young women
like beautiful possibilities in the world.

Hands move over piano keys, a song lifts
and we're undone in that moment,
the music runs on, green days spinning,
there's no standing aside and we're speechless.

Somewhere around here all the imagery is abandoned,
stubborn, it litters the ground, and I see you step around it.

Hearing Mishearing Doug Oliver

1 The Owners' Enclosure

Though some raiders will die, we could surround this place,
block the exits, take the rooftops and scope the winner on the plinth,
the lizard faced millionaire in duck-shit-green tweeds and pointy shoes.

Imagine the panic, the crowd as plural arrows convulsed and streaming;
he's in securities, he's in transport and this man combs the jumps:
we could call it *Killing the Rich at Play*, set that one dangling by a trope.

PR demands we don't harm the horses, the beautiful horses;
feel the thunder, see their bellies and legs full stretch over fences,
hear that gliding moment like a line cast out in an arc on still water.

Another problem: the Hussars are here in ceremonial costume and tall hats,
with their comrades away in Helmand, they're on big black fuck-off chargers;
if you imagine a troop of them advancing, at Peterloo say, history will falter.

That disenfranchisement will rise in your children's hearts like death;
so although some raiders will die, we have the taking of this place,
reduced here to transparent terms and moral confidence—off you go.

2 The Vaccination Queue

I queued at the surgery for the flu vaccination. I was with the old, saw
our ageing and I got it. We trailed out of the building and accepted
our parts as extras in a British comedy. A queue is an opportunity to be
orderly, anxious and complain in the service of humour.

—Look it says here, if you are breast feeding or trying to become
pregnant, tell the nurse.
—Well, I think you're safe then Edie.
—This is like the army. They didn't keep the needles sharp, just jabbed
'em in you and off you go to Timbuktu.

Most of the women shouted at most of the men.
—He can't hear me. Stand there, just wait. You're a bit deaf aren't you.

Many were the respectable poor, who no longer exist in any political discourse. They wear cheap clothes; the men in pressed grey trousers and thin brown slip-ons; the women in sensible three quarter length coats and shapeless slacks. You queue up because it's free—and they have paid all their lives. So they act sniffy, like a posh hat on humility. I'm at home with them and try to be helpful.

I remembered my mother talked about the doctor visiting. He arrived on a horse.
—He was so tall up there, he'd shout down at you all of your personal business, everybody heard. He was a kind old soul though.
A doctor making house visits on a horse? Have I made this up or read it in the sort of novel I don't read?

One winter my dad came off his bike, cracked his head, staggered home delirious and collapsed through the door. She tried to lift him up, saw the blood, shrieked and dropped him smack down on the flagstones. Later, the doctor, discretely dismounted, asked if she'd tried to kill him—I'd understand Mrs Corcoran but all the same, best not.

I suppose the accident of him not dying on this occasion, and the succession of generations, drops me in this queue. It helps me stand here and shuffle forward. I imagine every one of us standing here must be informed by such events—like a bright axis of personal identity intersecting the queue unseen and unheard. Our queue, snaking back through history via Beveridge, the Empire and beyond, is of course the English class system as vernacular drama. You know your place and how to behave, thank you. Nobody waiting for the vaccination pushed; one man faking confusion, cheated. The general disapproval unspoken hung in the air we all breathed.

3 The Harbour Open to all of the World

The pinman hero, half in half out of the water,
stretches ardent across the mouth of the harbour;
he's keeping the harbour open to the whole world,
if you could only believe he'd hold that posture.

Red faced expats walk and talk their foreign languages
and Albanian builders dance over the roof tiles;
a generation ago children walked down the mountain
and took the boat to school in Kardamyli.

There's evidence here of Neolithic settlement,
—did they paddle out in boats of stone, logs and leaves?
their art of carved bone dynamic and literal,
their rituals drove the seasons in their course.

Helen's brothers stood on that island there,
calming the waters as she fled with an astonished Paris;
after Actium Antony chased Cleopatra this way,
at last they spoke, then did sup and lie together.

The fishermen Christeas in the Argonautis putter out,
their outboard weaving sleep on the black water;
cast far like a string of pearls by merchants of the Morea
trade routes pour into the lap of the Serene Empire.

Out there subterranean streams emerge on the surface,
cold and still, a fresh water ellipse like a glassy eye
reducing the waves to a flickering circle;
becalmed we float in the origin of all our telling.

Looking back, the forgotten harbour stays open,
the whole world rolling in and out of its arms.

Byron's Karagiozis

This lake and town of Byron's escape
appears as fresh as a boy's face;
milord's playthings arrayed across the plain,
the shoreline stepping in and out of the ever living past.

The Pasha scans the mountain paths for rebels
rising to the blue of Ottoman heaven,
saunters along the landing strip of the unaligned
—my palace, my lands of blood, my lord—welcome.

We dropped out of thin air over the Pindhus,
a door opened became a flood of light;
landing gear scarring the face reflected
the water full of boats and sacked women.

This the first Albanian song of Lordy Viron,
the second a lamentation of unrequited love;
the clarinos sob sob, the real men howl
—ah your pink ears, their coral portal and lightshine.

⋆

Scene 1

Enter Spiridion Foresti, British Consul, dancing with the Governor of Malta, cloaked in smiles—'We can send young Byron to traverse the province, let him bind the Pasha by his vices to our cause, and just think how well it will be received—an Albanian front against Napoleon.'

'Does the young lord have to know? Reputation says he's of the same kind, he can be our Karagiozis, with a big fat cock to catch the devil.'
A paper boat bobs across the screen, the Spider, British warship, flags flying, and off goes Byron to Prevesa, dumb little thing in a puppet show.

⋆

The music is different village to village,
in my village Konitsa, it is lighter, other places
sadder—like the stone we build black or white,
the stone is just for that village, the right stone.

But the songs, most songs, all over about the same,
being away, not home, songs of away, to say exile,
as they play for you, you know Saturday, off work,
the longing of Albania or another Greece or Germania.

⋆

Eleftheria showed us the painted Ottoman door
taken from the dump, under the blackened surface
a blue green meadow of flowers and birds interwoven
flooding a lattice of apricots and pinks.

Idealised peony or rose, an eternal spring at the centre
the habitation of songbirds, rescued from the tip,
—we keep it here, not in our rooms, so all can see
and the colours of the house are taken from it.

⋆

From the capital of the East
two experimental cantos,
the minarets of Tepelene like meteorites
—who now shall lead the scattered children forth?

Journey made difficult by Ramadan and rain
nine hours lost in the storm at Zitza,
we lit fires, fired guns to find the party;
Byron, cloaked to his eyes, under a rock, content.

Remembered lowering coast and the name—Missolonghi,
dark mind on darker waters held silent;
Wahhabi's rebel brood, their pious spoil
a path of blood running to the west.

At Ioanina the houses and domes
glitter through gardens of lemon and orange trees,
the lake spreads itself from the cypress grove
making a track into a land of no fixed boundaries.

⸺ ★ ⸺

Scene 2

At the Karagiozis staged for Ramadan, Hobhouse and Byron agog;
on the other side of the art of the theatre of shadows
Captain Leake unloads guns and ammunition,
Ali Pasha enters, raises his eyebrows and pats the ordnance.

Byron skips on in Albanian finery, begins a letter—My Dear Mother,
he reveals to the audience an enormous penis strung from his neck;
straining, he soliloquises and beats the beast, rolling across the floor,
admiring his guest's performance, eyes alight, the Pasha approaches.

⸺ ★ ⸺

The stone villages rise and fall
as if abandoned on rolling Zagori,
we saw photographs of children
on the walls of all the tavernas.

Formal, dressed in white
for a festival in the platea,
rows and rows of children
from fifty years ago.

⸺ ★ ⸺

You must be quiet crossing the bridge,
stop the music, dismount and step softly.

Don't let the one sacrificed below
catch us at our wedding in this upper world.

If she hears the music she'll join the party,
the bridge collapse and we'll never cross over.

⋆

Scene 3

A large room paved with marble, a fountain playing at the centre, men lounge and suck sherbet; then to a rough fanfare painted boys in spinning circles sing 'Oh your curling hair and small ears.'—Ali, ornate craft borne aloft by many hands, responds profundo, 'You must think of me as a father, a father, a father.'

As the tide of seduction rises with pretty animals, sweetmeats and aerial Ali, the devil descends and affixes the monster penis to the image of every future lover, mistress, wife and sister of the alarmed poet: Byron darkens and grits his teeth, smoke form his burnt journals obscures the scene.

⋆

Streets dark all day, damp
tip tap from the dance school,
houses slumped in glutinous air
nothing for it but drown in the lake.

I am sick of vice, tried all its varieties,
it's time to leave off wine and carnal company
and betake myself to politics and decorum;
—a vast mountain that little word.

Then from the bazaar a wedding party dances,
her hat of gold coins, her face painted red and white,
the men singing—Erotica Erotica, a sweet song for ladies
echoes off the whole world, the girl in coins glinting.

Looking at you what language is left?

The passes we travelled have left a river running in my heart.

The dragomen were silent crossing the bridges.

In that small bay Antony lost the world.

⋆

The Albanian girls circle the square
on bikes borrowed from the Ingalish,
—thank you, thank you, we bring back,
silver spokes turning spindly legs push.

They circle under the tower's long shadow
and the day darkens for time to stop,
the mountains come falling down falling down
and the world walks away on terraced light.

⋆

Scene 4

On this side of the art of the theatre of shadows
Ali Pasha is beheaded by his Ottoman masters in 1822,
the blue and white flags of a new nation flood the land
and Byron, poster boy in exile, would lead the children forth.

⋆

By morning we woke in the bowl of mountains,
snowbound peaks shining up the sky chemicals
of the big fat day on its feet and shouting.

The clarino rising wails—what word, what root will break
the rock wolves in rounds, heads back sing, pelts spark
black Zagori night unveils the first light of another country.

Epicurus Is My Neighbour

He was the son of economic migrants,
the borders had holes in then, the bosses forgetful;
there were compensations on Samos—and fish.

He recruited his brothers as his first adherents,
and seeking undisturbedness he travelled widely:
Samos; Athens; Colophon; Mytilene and Lampsacus.

A car lights the dark road running,
we thought of the towns out there, subtle objects
in motion—the infinite as absence of collision.

Epicurus walked out on nonsense and uncaring gods,
let it come to us by this light, he sat in his garden,
written on carbonised papyrus, chipped in stone.

*

We're walking by the sea Melanie,
the sea's full of stories, wavering and drunk,
the olive trees whirl and stars like spilt milk.

The light slides over the water once only,
below it's dark, all the way down unthinkable,
—so don't think about it then, you'd say.

Let's walk to the house, it's after the next turn,
the air fit medium for the colour shift of night.

*

Epicurus stands at the door of the sea,
he fixes his mouth in place, sea-foam
forms an outline like fuzzy television,
the trick is to read it as a poem.

I'm not making this up, Epicurus
waits for the fat snow to fall,
to calculate the disposition of the flakes
the dance of sensory data around the world.

*

Another night in, storm rocking the lamp
the red wine I think, roast potatoes, onion,
readings from Lucretius and a slight moon;
the sky falling away like a dreaming face,
a girl's face looking out to sea, eyes open.

We drove down through swirling fog,
Langada, Thalames, the mountain made invisible,
the roads in Sparta like black rivers run,
a Spring tide of black glass splintering
the roots and names of big gods and little gods.

With morning up early for Clean Monday
the kites sail high as white on blue,
a white word disintegrating the whole sky
keeps us fed, makes us free, let's me sit here
and stare at the green gate to the sea.

*

I saw a completeness it made sense I was a boy and it was death I saw their faces	but would not step away please not yet then my girls then two women looking down
but would not step away please not yet then my girls then two women looking down	I saw a completeness it made sense I was a boy and it was death I saw their faces

*

Herodotus before you run me down in Athens
let me give you a summary of my system.
Ataraxia: I've stretched it on a banner across the street
          ATARAXIA
for all to pass under and gaze upon in wonder.

There's no point in using words that make no sense,
that are unattached to the world; we know it, everyday
we know it, that's apparent despite the same old business;
look at the boundless sky—and my banner,
look at boundlessness at every turn, bodies and void.

      *

The wind blows and the house stands,
the roof holds and I see us lie under it;
I see the garden thrashing all night and
the village launch itself into deep water,
the wind rolling off the sea explodes thought.

In mountain clamour the high meadows
blown white and bare detonate particles at swim
against our silver window, a lexicon
smashed and scattered uncoded bright beads
remaking the swept world by morning.

Mountains rise in the empty box of the sky,
the fresh green smell of sap fills the air
and if there's talk around here, it won't trouble
the stealthy ships of an unknown country
rounding the headland in silence.

      *

a body of fine particles
dispersed
          furthermore

the birds in the bare tree
the birds in the green leafy

furthermore
the mode of investigation counts

attend to the visible
a bound or outer limit set

a single account is the business of those
who wish to perform marvels for the rabble

Thales invented water—Epicurus ease
he danced with Lucretius

Madeleine's Letter to Bunting

Day 1

The year goes out in a high wind,
sunlight steps across the floor in stripes
and various animals come around for food.

The sea charges petrol blue and lucid,
the whole garden dancing at night
unparades me cat and black sleep owl.

I can see the red hibiscus in darkness,
I read your poem Letter to Bunting,
the start of the dream, in amazement.

Day 2

Sun lights the end of the year
the wind has dropped to nothing
Benazir Bhutto has been shot.

We dug experimental holes around the house,
broke a spade and hoe on buried rock
planted songlines, a lemon tree and shrubs.

Sixty Kenyans incinerated in a church
I climbed into the eucalyptus, swinging
through the world like a bug on a blade of grass.

The sea all around on three sides glows,
I grasped the springy boughs in my useless arms
I smelt good and hung on against sense.

This tree has such a colour,
is it blonde cinnamon, and the etymology?
—she might sweep me up if I fall.

At your age I thought I had a plan,
I did not, or it was the wrong plan;
it was not to be fifty and exhausted up a tree.

Speaking the only three words I have
to the local children bemused,
arms numb—Eucalyptus, if I fall, save me.

Day 3

Took the tallest branches out,
hit the supply cable on the way down,
same sun, same sea and dizzying view.

Face covered in scented sawdust
dancing the ladder tiptoe around the trunk,
no power, no light, no heating, no food.

Five cats and a dog came to be fed,
smoke drifted into the empty harbour
a bowl of smoke from the olive harvest.

Raked out the weeds and undergrowth
around the new shrubs, found a snakeskin;
how the roots take I don't know.

Anchored to rocks, strong white fingers
cling to the underground life,
only the radio news is fatal.

Later, after eating in Agios Nicholaos,
a fishing boat dressed in Christmas lights
would look good out on the water.

Day 4

High wind roaring all night,
read until 3 a.m.—woke to broken sun,
the whole village in its morning dance.

The sea turned a metallic grey
white riders outward bound,
a sound like understanding just born.

My lemon tree looks bonny in the breeze,
we walked over terraces, olive trees
flickering green and white, to see neighbours.

Dionysus has been sighted
all along this coast, the rocks speak
the rivers run his name.

Away cold brother of white thought,
what season sits on your back
over mountains covered in Spring.

She went away one night, left
the children whispering at the door,
her eyes empty, her mind leaping.

And at that, the bright green shoots
pierced our feet and hands to tap tap,
Dionysus rising answers—I want to.

Day 5

Madeleine, my unabashed girl, I'm saying this to you,
because of your poem—Letter to Bunting;
you already have the trick of writing from the body,
of not explaining that you are you and not you in the poem

but trust to the shape and weight of words as you go;
there's no passport for the journey you might take,
just breathing each beat, a young woman breathing
says—snake I want to be bit a little.

Day 6

Has the making of a halcyon day,
the kingfisher safe front holds
what blue the sea has taken on,
as barely tidal music surrounds us;
we sat and played stare-cat with the dogs,
the sunlight dreams an early spring
like the first morning of a new life.

Last night we went to the harbour at midnight,
fireworks explode, children singing St Basil
to bless the houses of the living;
the priest and the policeman danced together
and the old year tipped into the new,
quick fire shooting across black water
binding the time to set us free.

We could launch the ship of lights
out into the Neolithic darkness,
learn the many conditions of the sea
and sail south around Cape Matapan;
a risen world in that first moment lifts
the candid islands of lyric and rock and sky
from the Aegean heart of all our making.

Day 7

Between etymon and Eucharist
gum-tree, I am stuck up a,
to get a text from you on Euro Star.

Saw the fire damage around Paradesia,
hills folded in ash, hills shadowing hills,
miles of it like burnt black hair.

At 30,000 feet out of my tree I
smack into an endless England,
the tendentious politics of a small island.

Beneficial in destroying the miasma
of malarias districts, I swing
wrapped around the trunk.

On the Xenophone Label

Propositions 1

On the Xenophone label
crackling late at night
from the outpost barbarians in the hills
at the beginning as one

*

That these fossils prove
the earth was once sea
my eye on the substance
the whole world one god

*

What men think they know
is no more than the impulse
of frogs gathered around a puddle
singing late into the Spring night

*

From Syracuse Dear Parmenides
the sun is new every day
the sea has covered the land bridge
and the clouds ignite by motion

*

The limits of human knowledge
do not excuse inquiry
you are not off the hook
the rim of the world burning

*

The roots of the earth
and the unharvested sea
are above Tartarus the fool knows
set forth from Colophon unmapped

*

Religion makes men hungry
they sing pray parade up and down
then crowd the taverna their shiny faces
take eat take eat the whole world

*

In this airy space unconfined
I was not Homer's boy
I was not a mouth for hire
amber set fast about my buzzing words

*

In the chapters of sweetness
yellow honey gods made figs
made all things clear
iambic frogs meteors first principles

*

Empirical root holds true
thus I in rhapsody
at the edge of the dark sea
saw the town of men wake to light

*

Not plague nor Harpagus
but mumbo jumbo mytho Pytho

brings down the city
bang bang you thought wrong

*

And with my own eyes
silver jackal black snake
green lizard spring I saw
all things with my own eyes

*

At first I heard the name
Xenophanes of Colophon
middle up middle down
the music of reason Xenophanes

A Biography of Xenophanes

Son of Dexus or Dexinos or Orthomenes
against Homer
against Hesiod
against Pythagoras
outlived his sons
defender of the city

Gadfly of Ionia, Sicily, Italy
gadfly against false wisdom
inquired into meteors, eclipses
fishes whirlwinds religion
the shape and location of the Earth
the substance of all existing things

inquirer into moderation of conduct

Greetings 1

Parmenides my friend when
did we last speak how
are you and the horses and
your straight purpose I
am variously employed
in the many Greek lands
to make a living away
from home observed fact
came to call this morning
a warm wind of ignition
stirred the endless sea was
once land and my mind turned
to you in the market place
fresh melons that day off
the boat their liquid knock
as they collide caused an
argument atoms at war the
language of thirst exploded
one combatant quoted your
sharp mind like a knife
melons rolling everywhere
thuk thuk percussion subtle
as honey in sunlight a riot
you recall that day when
unmediated Harpagus
drove us westward the tide
the counter tide turns how
long do you think what is it
in such abandonment my
whole life strung out on wires
rigged the journeys made
lucid sea lanes of the
objective case a marvel
of song imagine song spun
around the earth even as

this letter beats its path
to you there's lightning
out on the waves revelation
along a long tunnel of
sound flooded the harbour
physis a chamber of noise
to knock me down the world
abides no less I saw one
moment the burning map
fire walking on water
they say that once sap
from pine bacchants of
pine in the air around the
house the voice and clatter
of gods they say
a voice in the resinous
body of night of earth
articulated a thesis
rising in a sort of song.

Biography 2

Only poetry can do this
from an island invaded
by the world   only poetry
to the west Greek earthed

Xenophanes came here
his eyes open he walked
through the valley of temples
followed by twenty dogs

Thought sharp at first light
reverence   scepticism
opened his eyes on an island
of white marble Aegean

The cypress the mimosa
the fluted columns rose
from the same impulse
Xenophanes first saw this.

Propositions 2

Number magic is as useful as
a dog barking in the early hours
there's nothing to steal here
only sanctimonious cant

*

Men's heads   melons
inside secret wet flesh
thinking: thuk thuk?
judged by action—who can say?

*

Let's talk of the old days in
Colophon when the hexameters
ignited first thoughts and we stood
together in the innocent air

*

Saw a kingfisher flash
green fire low on the water
in the still air of the harbour
nothing of earth about it

*

Black is their new purple
they crowd the market conjure
an empire of denial magazine hair
oh but I am not interested in this passing world etc etc

*

The usefulness of fruit
as analogous to men
may be limited however
melons are less dense

*

The old women sit out
in the slow evening talk
eat they might sing float
away over the dark mountains

*

Up in the western market early for
weapons systems a new dawn
effaces an ethical consideration
holy script written in blood—yours

*

The sea beaten out silver
surrounds the children's dark heads
bobbing in family groups
their likeness—another message

*

Whispered in schools sung from towers
at dawn by rote in the blood
repeated in the houses of power
dog barking sanctimonious cant

*

To think with darkness abroad
the whole world but one constant

oh my drowned friends all
lost in the bloody roots of reason

⁂

The local bees here are black
heavy hanging in the yasmina
even the little white stars come
spinning down to earth from the earth

⁂

post-Eleatic clean out of memory
1 earth 2 water 3 sun 4 return
= the moist ground of we who come into being
Gaia 1 2 3 4 ends up Gaia

Biography 3

The idea shone like static in his mind
as bright as 92 summers in the Greek lands
as morning rolled out to claim its origin
and the seas and rivers exhaled the balmy night.

Watching the shadows run to ground
he thought of the visible, the uncontained,
reason fighting upstream on an ordinary day
as a boy where he stood in the land first lost.

Orchards of cherry trees, silver traced in white rock,
there is one source—constant and the same—
the conflict of interest is real enough,
their mouths big and slack with wealth.

What age were you when the Mede came,
when the sea invaded the land and left its mark?
Image of seaweed, a fish in the quarries at Syracuse,
a bay-leaf print deep in Parian marble.

Greetings 2

Parmenides the Eleatic sun
has hammered my brain shut
beaten flat the mountains and sea
to an oily picture of nothing
in a white hot squint I saw
the village idiot bring the news
he held up a letter and showed
all of us pointing at the black
headlines given the way it goes
he's the best messenger we have
look it says cynical butchers
revenge comes to roost blah the
blah bosses emblazon power on
shiny coins like miniature shields
hoarded in darkness their
commerce but war by another
name the world will end because
of a, b or c or any combination
of private armies skulk in the hills
eyeing up the port for a, b or c
the night barely dissolved at dawn
the tradesman arrive singing
the dogs barking loop the loop
dive under the donkeys kick up
biting the tassels choral yelps
you want these onions this pot
you sure want this cure make her
love you all night everything moving
against everything and the children
chase the dogs the mothers scream
from the yards the men shout
what is going on how can I
pray for a rent cut with all this
fucking noise it is a perfect model
of the One morning stark

the idiot can explain the lot
my brain as I've said is shut
the work comes and goes
the Big Idea holds true
I tote it about the dusty circuit
slip and slide drink the lord's wine
eat at his fat-faced table you want
this thought this lesson on human
understanding everything knocks
against everything the mighty hymn
of substance thuk thuk you know
the verb in Homer designates
the reaching of the water up to
Tantalus' chin and the action
of the waves warding off snowflakes
we're up against it   the world
of land and sea that lies all
about us   there   that's it   picture
me   mouth open   just above
the rising tide of matter   talking

Biography 4

After what should be talked about
had been talked about, the men were quiet,
at rest, fed and lounging.

The girl sang into the still night,
Xenophanes was not old then, the years fell away,
the experience complete in itself.

She stood amongst them in their woven garlands,
looking ahead, unabashed and beautiful
—there was no philosophy for it.

It would take 2000 years
for this moment to be understood,
no-one spoke, the distance held.

O mediatrix clemens, O Beatrice,
a girl floating to the shore
steps through the door into light.

The End of It All

Plato's thought police and their like would not have it:
for espousing that the heavenly bodies are not gods
bent on doing only what is best Xenophanes would get
five years solitary and for its repetition—the chop.

How gentle is the exploration of the limits of human knowledge;
from inside such inquiry, a faint ghost in an empty land, we hear
a transparent whisper of almost nothing through another's history,
we're not even there and the imperial circus of claimants presses.

Exiled to the roadhouse circuit—stubborn, sceptical, unassigned,
Xenophanes saw one night the cold stars in a presentive sky,
heard the dogs barking tuneful nonsense village to village
and entered the network of the brimming world.

Propositions 3

The invention of coinage
and Lydian luxury   retail
gone to hell in a handcart
prepared the ground for invasion

*

When I turned around
the garden's green shade
a thin green snake
whipped across my feet

*

At night two villages away
—who calculated the intervals?-
of perfect quarter tones   the east
calling home in the blood

*

The heat that summer
killed the cicadas stone dead
power trembling on the air
the mirage of harbour defences

*

My children in another land
my days are dust   stop
going around the Greek cities
to follow the money   stop

*

Anthropomorphic fallacy
eucalyptus bee dust sky
blue sky another house *agathon*
sing up little sparrow sing up

*

The new wine of Elea is sharp
but softens the gathering night
as the memory of small fires
makes the sun rise every day

*

The branches the limbs
of the celebrants surround my house
against divination fact finding
made me partisan of the One

*

My hands deep in the logic
of our present language
a spring candid and common
others will come to unearth

*

The honey-sweet wine
returns us to the earth
first light stumbling block
of the lower town in glory

*

Champion of infinite logic
captain of the steady state

all things are one in Catana
running to the edge of knowing

⭑

During eruption and earthquake
they believe priests wrapped in smoke
take the clamorous crowd as teacher
lest the ground open and mean nothing

⭑

In the light of either 'into' or
'in' or 'to' earth (or the earth)
taken as head to foot
exact as human knowledge

Notes

From Where Song Comes
See Hugh MacDiarmid 'In Memoriam James Joyce', Maurice Bowra *Primitive Song* and John Blacking *How Musical Is Man*.

Reading *The Cantos*
Morritt who reports on the generosity of Captain Christeas is J.B.S. Morritt in *A Grand Tour: Letters and Journeys 1794–96*.

From the Hen-Roost
The epigraph is from E. Pound.

A Thesis on the Ballad
The quotation in 'The Truth' is from M.J.C. Hodgart, *The Ballads*.

News of Aristomenes
The only sustained source for the figure of Aristomenes, scourge of the Spartans, is Pausanias. See also Daniel Ogden *Aristomenes of Messene: Legends of Sparta's Nemesis*. With thanks to Alistair Noon.

The Family Carnival
Some of the carnival songs can be found on the CD *Carnival Songs: The Sacred in the Profane* from The Greek Folk Music Association.

Byron's Karagiozis
The idea that Byron was used as sexual bait for Ali Pasha, to win allegiance to the British cause in the conflict with Napoleon, can be found in Ian Gilmour's *The Making of the Poets: Byron and Shelley in Their Time*.

Epicurus Is My Neighbour
Anything remotely to do with Epicurus in this poem comes from Eugene O'Connor's translation *The Essential Epicurus: Letters, Principal Doctrines, Vatican Sayings, and Fragments*.

On the Xenophone Label
Sources include J. H. Lesher: *Xenophanes of Colophon: Fragments: A Text and Translation with Commentary*; George Thompson: *The First Philosophers: Studies in Ancient Greek Society* and Sherod Santos: *Greek Lyric Poetry*.

www.ingramcontent.com/pod-product-compliance
Lightning Source LLC
Chambersburg PA
CBHW031158160426
43193CB00008B/431